FARM ANIMALS

PIGS

by Sheri Doyle

raintree
a Capstone company — publishers for children

Raintree is an imprint of Capstone Global Library Limited, a company incorporated in England and Wales having its registered office at 264 Banbury Road, Oxford, OX2 7DY – Registered company number: 6695582

www.raintree.co.uk
myorders@raintree.co.uk

Edited by Erika L. Shores
Designed by Ashlee Suker
Picture research by Marcie Spence
Production by Eric Manske

ISBN 978 1 4747 1906 3
20 19 18 17 16 15
10 9 8 7 6 5 4 3 2 1

Photo Credits
Corbis: Russ Munn/AgStock Images, 11; Dreamstime: Mantonino, 9, Martinedegraaf, 17; fotolia: Lyrk, 7; iStockphoto: BertBeekmans, 13, Rhoberazzi, 19; Shutterstock: Galyna Andrushko, 5, jokter, cover, 1, Lynne Carpenter, 21, Vphoto, 15

We would like to thank Gail Saunders-Smith, PhD, and Dr. Celina Johnson for their invaluable help in the preparation of this book.

Note to Parents and Teachers

This book describes and illustrates pigs. The images support early readers in understanding the text. The repetition of words and phrases helps early readers learn new words. This book also introduces early readers to subject-specific vocabulary, which is defined in the Glossary section. Early readers may need assistance to read some words and to use the Table of contents, Glossary, Read more, Internet sites and Index sections of the book.

Printed and bound in China.

Contents

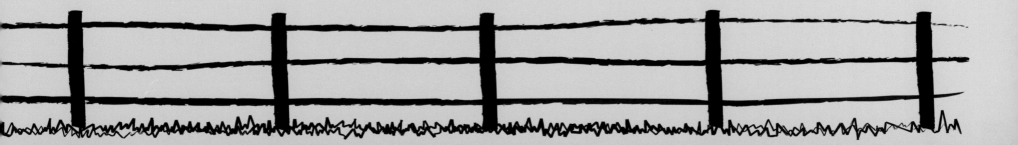

Meet the pigs

The morning sun shines

on the farmyard.

Oink! Here come some pigs!

They sniff the ground

with their snouts.

Pigs have thick bodies covered in hair. Some pigs have ears that stick up. Others have floppy ears. Pigs walk on sturdy hoofs.

On the farm

Pigs eat feed made from corn,

soybeans and other food.

Some pigs graze

in fenced pastures.

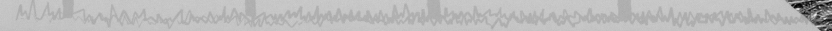

When pigs get very big,
they are called hogs.
Farmers raise hogs for
their meat.

Some hogs grow to be
454 kilogrammes (1,000 pounds)
or more. That's as heavy as
a grand piano!

New life

Eight piglets are born!

They squeal and drink milk.

Females grow up to be sows.

Males are called boars.

Pigs can live for 15 years.

Playtime

Pigs are smart and playful.

Some farmers give pigs balls

to play with.

Happy pigs grunt.

The midday sun is strong.

Pigs cannot sweat.

They roll in mud puddles

to stay cool.

Time to rest

Pigs sleep in barns.

They snuggle on floors

padded with straw.

Glossary

boar adult male pig

feed food that comes in the form of mash or pellets

graze eat grass

hog male pig that is raised for meat and weighs over 102 kilogrammes (225 pounds)

hoof pig's foot

pasture grassy area that pigs and other animals feed on

snout pig's nose

sow adult female pig

Read more

Farm Animals (World of Farming), Nancy Dickmann (Raintree, 2011)

Farm Animals: True or False? (True or False?), Daniel Nunn (Raintree, 2013)

The Barnyard (Animal World), Cody McKinney (Capstone Press, 2015)

Websites

discoverykids.com/category/animals/
Learn facts about animals and check out photos of all sorts of animals on this website.

kids.nationalgeographic.com/animals
Search for different sorts of animals and learn where they live, what they eat and more.

Index

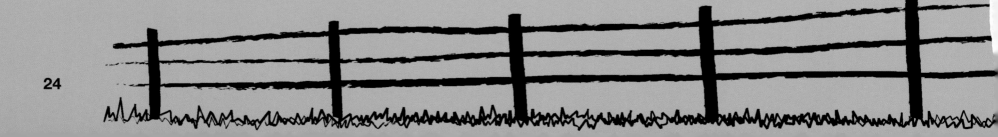